STORM STRUCK

WHEN SUPERCHARGED WINDS SLAMMED NORTHWEST MICHIGAN

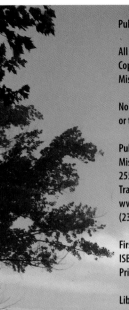

Published by Mission Point Press

Published by
Mission Point Press
2554 Chandler Road
Traverse City, Michigan 49696
www.MissionPointPress.com
(231) 421-9513

First edition, first printing
ISBN: 978-1-943995-00-4
Printed in the United States of America.

Library of Congress Control Number: 2015949894

Introduction and narrative by Robert Campbell
Storm Struck: When Supercharged Winds Slammed Northwest Michigan

Book design and photography editing by Heather Lee Shaw
Photographic captions edited by Bob Butz
Narrative edited by Doug Weaver
Cover photo by Sara Kassien
Backcover photo by Jim Anderson
Title photo by Coast Guard Lt. Cmdr. Charter Tschirgi
Photo this page by Jeff Herman
Map by Colleen Zanotti

Photographs provided by citizens and visitors of the Northwest Michigan region.
Photograph copyrights remain with the photographers.

 MISSION POINT PRESS

A Crowd-Sourced Book from the Community
Following a social media blast by Mission Point Press, more than 70 local or visiting photographers submitted their visions of the storm, resulting in well over 300 photographs from Leelanau County, Traverse City, Old Mission Peninsula, Acme, Williamsburg, Alden, Frankfort, and Emmet, Kalkaska, and Antrim counties.

For every paperback sold, Mission Point Press will donate $1 to the Friends of Sleeping Bear Dunes for forest and trail restoration.

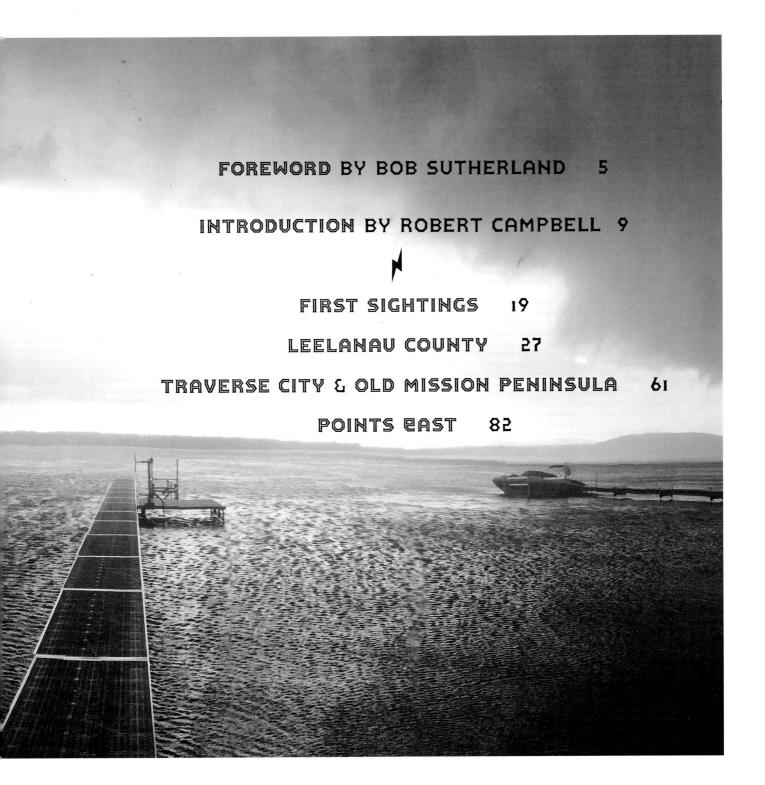

FOREWORD BY BOB SUTHERLAND   5

INTRODUCTION BY ROBERT CAMPBELL 9

FIRST SIGHTINGS   19

LEELANAU COUNTY   27

TRAVERSE CITY & OLD MISSION PENINSULA   61

POINTS EAST   82

Old Mission Peninsula, Grand Traverse County
Photo by Barbara Weber
"My nephew lives in Florida and kept saying to my dad,
'This is sad. Papa, I think we're going to need a new tree.
Maybe we should go back to Florida. Or the basement.'"

I am sitting outdoors under a great white oak as I write this. It is one of the proud survivors that stand among his fallen brothers. Both oak and I are stunned at the severity of the destruction; Glen Arbor's great white oaks took the brunt of this bewildering storm.

We were 20 miles south when the storm hit. As we approached home, up M-22, we first saw overturned docks and loose boats on the southwest side of Little Glen Lake. Then the massive cottonwoods in front of Glen Lake Manor, uprooted ... fallen flat, with giant root balls hanging in the air.

We drove across The Narrows between the Glen lakes. Trees seemed intact, but M-22 was backed up going into Glen Arbor at the intersection of Sunset Road. We stepped out of the car to wait, and soon friends surrounded us. Harry Fried was in subtle shock. He had walked ahead to see what the stoppage was and saw that hundreds of trees were laying across M-22. "No chance we make it into GA this way," Harry said.

So we ditched our car to hike the two short miles through the deep woods of Alligator Hill, where we hoped to reach home sweet home.

It wasn't 15 minutes before we realized the challenge ahead. Before us, as far as we could see, was a swath of fallen giants, jumbled like scattered fencerows. We climbed and crawled, over and under, at an infant's pace.

At last we reached the high, northwest side of the Alligator and saw sweeping views of Sleeping Bear Bay and Big Glenn Lake — views that hadn't been seen since the loggers of the 1880s cut this hillside to the dirt.

This storm — this incredible, devilish, harrowing, 100-mph combination of wind and hail — had cut a deep and wide clearing through the Alligator's thick forest. Below us, like a felled army, lay an impenetrable mix of uprooted oaks and beeches, snapped in half or worse, their giant, broken splinters pointing to the brightening sky.

We were stunned. None of us had seen destruction like this before. That it happened to this land that we hold so sacred tripled the pain. My wife, Steph, and I shared a moment together with moist eyes and soft hearts.

This book chronicles, in a small way, the tragedy that was this storm. Yes, the destruction started in Glen Arbor. But it moved swiftly east to ravage other lands, other homes, other lives. So it's not a Glen Arbor story alone. It's much more.

It also would be wrong to wallow in the pain. Because this storm brought out the best in us. We're Northwest Michiganders, after all. What doesn't kill you makes you stronger, they say. It's true.

So you'll also see stories and photographs in these pages of heroes, of communities pulling together, of strength and endurance. Even some laughter among the tears.

A bit later that afternoon, while walking with my son Colebrook, we paused along a road. Colebrook pointed happily to a giant white oak. The oak held the rope that he and our other son Hawthorn had liked so much for swinging. Back then I'd push them along when they were barely able to hold on. The oak stood tall, unscathed.

It was good that Colebrook shared a positive story by pointing to a survivor. He will be OK; so will I. So will Glen Arbor. He will never forget this experience; he'll save it to tell his grandkids and maybe yours as well. His stories will have happy endings as trees grow, and buildings repair, and landscapes fill out. As with all the great natural places, beauty always wins in the end.

—Bob Sutherland is the founder and president of Cherry Republic in Glen Arbor

Cherry Republic and the Utopia Foundation have launched a "Bring the Arbor Back to Glen Arbor" fundraising campaign—a reforestation project. For information, go to cherryrepublic.com and click on "Bob's Blog."

LAKE MICHIGAN

N

THE SCIENCE OF THE STORM

Unstable air caused by a combination of warm temperatures and moisture formed a "bow-echo" storm just before it hit Glen Arbor. In such a storm, warm, moist air drifts up to levels of 10,000 to 20,000 feet above the Earth's surface. That then sucks down fast-moving winds in the upper atmosphere, and the result is a severe thunderstorm with powerful, straight-line winds. Radar showed the storm moving over a broad area, but the greatest damage was along a narrower path that varied from 10 to 15 miles wide as it moved from the west-northwest to the east-southeast.

Charlevoix

Norwood

Eastport

Torch Lake

North Manitou Island

South Manitou Island

Northport

Grand Traverse Bay

Leland

Omena

Suttons Bay

Old Mission

Central Lake

Little Traverse Lake

Glen Arbor ❸

❷

Glen Lake

Lake Leelanau

West Bay

East Bay

Lake Bellaire

❶

❺

❹

❻

❼

Elk Rapids

❶❶

Empire

Yuba ❾

Acme

Traverse City ❽

❶❷

❶❷

❶❷

Rapid City

Lake Skegemog

Platte Lake

Crystal Lake

Frankfort

Kalkaska

STORM BY THE NUMBERS

■ PEAK WINDS: 100 mph, confirmed in Glen Arbor

■ DEATHS: None

■ SERIOUS INJURIES: At least three, including two men who had to be transported by boats to reach ambulances.

■ HAIL: Largest hailstone ever in northern Mi: Ogemaw County, 4.25"

■ DAMAGE IN LEELANAU COUNTY: $23.9 million

■ DAMAGE IN GRAND TRAVERSE COUNTY: $15.2 million

■ AGRICULTURAL LOSSES: "Many millions of dollars" (Michigan State University Extension)

A DESTRUCTIVE PATH

Weather officials called it a "bow echo," a bow-shaped storm usually found in states like Kansas and Missouri but rarely this far north. And it packed a wallop — straight-line winds up to 100 mph that cut a destructive path through the Grand Traverse region.

WHERE IT HIT HARD:

1 Sleeping Bear Dunes National Lakeshore: Hard-hit areas included the D.H. Day Campground, where all 88 camping sites were occupied; the top of Alligator Hill, where the equivalent of five football fields of trees were flattened; and the Sleeping Bear Heritage Trail, especially about 1.5 miles between Glen Arbor and Glen Haven.

2 Glen Arbor Township: Damage was widespread, but especially on the north shore of Glen Lake and the opposite shoreline (west of Burdickville). At least 20 boats were flipped upside down on the lake. One of the storm's most serious accidents occurred near the eastern end of the lake.

3 Village of Glen Arbor: Many people who had been shopping and eating were trapped by downed trees and live wires. The town hall provided temporary shelter; the chef and owner of the restaurant Blu provided more than 100 duck confit dinners.

4 Little Traverse Lake: Property near the lake's northeastern end had the most damage.

5 Area Around 45 North Winery: Although most of the storm's damage was to the south, this area, along the storm's northern edge, also was hit.

6 Peninsula Drive: The storm raked the trees surrounding bayside homes, from Munson nearly all the way to Bowers Harbor.

7 Along Bluff Road: Subdivisions here were struck hard, and as were areas farther south toward the base of Old Mission.

8 Along Munson Avenue: Many trees were uprooted, from South Garfield Avenue east to the community of Acme.

9 Acme To Yuba: The storm's epicenter crossed East Bay and came back onshore in an area from Acme to Yuba. Heavy damage occurred to orchards on and near Elk Lake Road south of Elk Rapids.

10 Skegemog Point: Severe property damage was sustained at the northern tip of the point along both Elk and Skegemog waterfront.

11 Skegemog, Torch Lakes: The storm continued along Fairmont Drive (on the north shore of Skegemog Lake), Torch River Drive (Torch River) and Crystal Beach on the south end of Torch Lake.

12 South of Rapid City: Winds raked areas near Rapid City Road, destroying many trees; a red-pine plantation was left bent at an extreme angle.

7

It was late afternoon on a steamy Sunday in early August.

Tens of thousands of locals, summer residents and tourists were enjoying their Up North lives — at Michigan beaches and dunes, at the final afternoon of the Traverse City Film Festival, at the wineries of the Leelanau and Old Mission peninsulas, and at homes, cottages and campgrounds across the region.

Some were keeping a prudent eye on the weather. Forecasts for Aug. 2 called for several waves of summer thunderstorms to move through northern Michigan.

Just before noon, a storm with winds estimated at up to 60 mph knocked down trees and power lines near Suttons Bay. About 45 minutes later, a storm with similar wind speeds wrought havoc around Burt and Mullett lakes, from Indian River to Cheboygan.

But a bigger, crueler monster was brewing offshore, above Lake Michigan. As it approached the Leelanau County shoreline, meteorologists saw the telltale bulge on their radar screens of a bow echo storm. Along the shoreline, hundreds of people photographed shelf clouds that had the look of Armageddon—an ominous cloud bank above deep green skies.

Bow echoes are rare in northern Michigan but well-known and much feared in states like Kansas, Missouri and Oklahoma — the nation's tornado alley. A bow echo develops when warm moist air rises 10,000 to 20,000 feet above the Earth's surface and changes the path of fast-moving upper atmosphere winds, channeling them at a sharp angle toward ground.

The result is straight-line winds with a shear force that can reach 100 mph, or more, and often deliver a punch over a much broader swath of land than a tornado. For perspective, consider that a 100 mph wind is the equivalent of an F1 tornado or a Category 2 hurricane.

At 3:57 p.m., the National Weather Service issued a severe weather warnings for Benzie, Leelanau, Grand Traverse, Manistee and Wexford counties (page 72). Minutes later, the storm slammed the shoreline along the Sleeping Bear Dunes National Lakeshore. Ravaging the land as it went, it marched swiftly east-southeast across Leelanau County towards West Bay. It then smashed through the southern half of Old Mission Peninsula and parts of Traverse City before charging across East Bay and battering the northwest corner of Grand Traverse County, including Elk and Skegemog lakes. It weakened at that point, but not before thrashing homes and forests in Kalkaska and Antrim counties.

M-37, Grand Traverse County
Photo by Marcia Wright
Vacationers heading to Glen Arbor along M-37 had no idea that all roads into the town were blocked. After being forced off the highway several times by driving rain, Marcia Wright captured this image of a black and ominous sky still hovering over Traverse City at around 7 p.m.

**Empire Beach,
Leelanau County
Photo by Shannon Rodgers**
Just before noon, after a morning of fishing with her 8-year-old son, Shannon Rodgers snapped this picture of Connor before the two took cover from the first storm that blew in over Lake Michigan.

Radar shows that as the storm moved, the bow echo became more pronounced — like an archer's weapon pulled taut. Indeed, the bow echo's winds would surge and smash and then, almost inexplicably, retreat upward. The pattern sometimes left one neighbor with extreme damage to home, outbuildings or vehicles as trees uprooted or snapped, while a next-door neighbor was spared but for a few downed limbs.

"It's such a chaotic formulation," said Bruce Smith, meteorologist in charge of the National Weather Service office in Gaylord. "It's certainly an event that northern Michigan doesn't see very often."

Smith was on the team that arrived in the days after the storm and confirmed wind speeds approaching 100 mph in Glen Arbor Township. Based on tree damage on Skegemog Point and Fairmont Drive, it's likely that winds of about the same speed struck there. Most of the downed trees lay in a west-northwest to east-southeast pattern. Smith said the difference in damage from 60 mph winds and 90–100 mph winds is enormous.

The wind speeds easily eclipsed Leelanau and Grand Traverse county records dating to 1950. They seemed almost biblical ... so fierce that they shoved the entire waters of Little Glen Lake hard to the east, dropping the west-side depth by 2 feet and temporarily creating beachfront that reached out at least 60 feet (page 52).

Many people near the storm's epicenter described the ferocious noise.

"It sounded like a train was coming down the street," said David Thomasma, owner of Synchronocity, an art gallery in Glen Haven.

Near the tip of Skegemog Point Road, on the peninsula which divides Elk and Skegemog lakes, Rob Kendall said that he first heard the deafening sound of the wind and hail, soon followed by the snapping and crashing of trees — 33 on his lot of about an acre.

"I was concerned that the end was nigh," he said. Five cars in or near his driveway were totaled, and the family's summer home suffered extensive damage.

His son, Adam, and new daughter-in-law, Kate, were married the day before at Samels Family Heritage Farm down the road, under an iconic oak tree where dozens of couples have said their vows over the decades. On Monday morning the tree lay on its side, snapped off at its trunk.

Besides the winds, the storm shot hailstones that ripped and punctured vines, grapes, trees, apples and other fruits. Elements of the same weather system brought the largest hailstone ever recorded in northern Michigan — 4.25 inches — to Clear Lake in Ogemaw County.

That not a single person died is perhaps the most remarkable outcome of the storm, as mature trees fell on homes, vehicles and power lines. Phrases like "grace of God," "incredible luck" and "it's a miracle" were used repeatedly to describe the absence of fatalities.

"I'm sure that if this had happened at night we would have had many fatalities," said Smith of the National Weather Service.

"It's unbelievable," said Joe Lachowski, a Sleeping Bear Dunes park ranger who was in charge of the emergency response on the night of the storm. At the park's D.H. Day Campground along the shoreline of Lake Michigan and just up the road from Glen Arbor, hundreds of trees fell on the 88 occupied campsites, flattening tents and badly damaging pop-up campers.

"We could have found that there were five or 10 fatalities in the campground," said Lachowski, "and no one would have been surprised given the severity of what we were seeing."

Atop Alligator Hill, a popular Lake Michigan overlook along a hiking trail in the Lakeshore, the storm delivered what was arguably its most brutal punch.

Matt Ansorge, the Leelanau County Emergency Management director, said an area the size of "four or five football fields" was mowed down. John Soderholm, the Glen Arbor Township supervisor, said it looked like a giant "had gone bowling in the forest."

Leelanau County
Photo by Donna Kaplowitz
"The crows know something is coming. "That is what Donna Rich Kaplowitz said to her son when she saw the crows perched atop a Port Oneida area barn around 11 a.m. on the day of the storm. The next day, as she captured more images of the devastation throughout the town and along M-22, she remembers feeling humbled by the power of Mother Nature and moved by how the community came together.

Amid the chaos of downed trees, darkness fell on five hikers stranded near the top of Alligator Hill. Using horns, lights and gunshots, park employees, sheriff's deputies and other emergency officials eventually directed the hikers to safety, but not until about 4 a.m. Monday morning.

Across the region, two of the most serious injuries occurred when trees fell on men in their cars — one a Colorado man driving to find his son near Glen Lake, the other a Massachusetts man who had come for the wedding on Skegemog Point.

In both instances, because ambulances couldn't reach them with so many fallen trees blocking roads, boats transported the men to ambulances that rushed them to Munson Medical Center in Traverse City. Both were released within a few days.

The photo of Carol Vernam's crushed '05 Volkswagen Beetle convertible (page 78) would convince anyone that no one in the car could have survived when the tree fell. Carol walked away after a conversation with God and assistance from three men who extracted her from her bug.

n Lake Michigan near South Manitou Island, a 33-year-old man was kayaking with his brother when he capsized after the storm hit. The brother made it to the island and called 911 on his cell phone. The victim was in 66-degree water for nearly six hours when he was spotted shining a flashlight as a Coast Guard search helicopter from the air station in Traverse City flew overhead. Minutes later, he was eased by a rescue swimmer into a basket and lifted into the chopper.

"He was shivering, alert, but he wasn't saying anything," said U.S. Coast Guard Lt. Commander Pablo Smith. If the man hadn't been wearing a life jacket, he would have died, Smith said.

Both Leelanau and Grand Traverse counties sought and received disaster declarations from the state. Ansorge of Leelanau County estimated property damage at $23.9 million, while his counterpart Gregg Bird in Grand Traverse County said damage totaled $15.2 million.

"I believe that this is going to be the costliest storm in the history of the county," Bird said.

On Glen Lake, at least 20 boats were overturned — mostly pontoons blown off their hoists. Damage was extensive, too, along the waterfronts to docks, hoists, canopies, boats and even a float plane on the Elk-Skegemog-Torch chain of lakes.

George Weeks, 83, who resides in Glen Haven and has lived in northern Michigan much of his life, said: "I was born and raised in Traverse City, and I've never seen anything like this. It's astounding that no one was killed."

Weeks, who remains a spokesman for former Michigan Gov. William Milliken, said the storm didn't even give the 93-year-old ex-governor a break, dropping trees across his driveway along West Bay on Old Mission Peninsula.

The county damage estimates don't include agricultural losses that are expected to be "many millions of dollars," said Duke Elsner, with the Michigan State University cooperative extension service office in Traverse City. Elsner, a small fruits expert, said: "This is the worst wind damage I've ever seen to vineyards, and the most storm damage I've seen in 25 years." The hail split open grapes and tore leaves off many vines.

"We'll be lucky if we get any crop," said Todd Oosterhouse of Bonobo Winery on Old Mission Peninsula.

Many orchard owners, especially in the apple and peach belt in Whitewater Township between East Bay and Elk Lake, said they lost all their fruit. In an older cherry orchard along Lossie Road, dozens of mature cherry trees were snapped off at their trunks.

It would be a lie to suggest that sparks of tension and anger didn't occur in the aftermath of the storm.

Park ranger Lachowski and Leelanau County Sheriff Mike Borkovich both said people who wanted to get away from the area or to their homes or cottages couldn't understand why roads were blocked. Downed trees and the potential for live, downed power lines were the reasons.

"A lot of people were in my face," Lachowski said. "They couldn't seem to understand that we were trying to prevent them from electrocuting themselves."

Conflicts also developed between utility and wood-cutting crews. The utility workers were trying to keep the storm-struck area secure while they worked to restore power. Meanwhile the wood cutters were responding to homeowners who had trees on their homes, Borkovich said.

"Overall, the people were great, though," he said, adding that many stopped at roadblocks with chainsaws or just bare hands, parked their vehicles and helped remove limbs and branches from the roads.

And while some storm victims seemed despondent in its aftermath, many showed resilience even as their homes were left heavily damaged or their shaded and cool retreats had become open, sunny lots pockmarked by stumps and root balls.

"Basically, it took out the forest around two sides of our house," said Bill Stott, who lives with his wife, Robbin, along Bluff Road in Peninsula Township on the Old Mission Peninsula. "We counted 16 root balls, two trees on

Leland, Leelanau County
Photo by Colleen Wares

"Van's Beach, approximately 3:55 p.m. This photo is a favorite. My grandson, Kyan Olshove, and I had gone to Leland for a minute and saw how the sky was changing, so we knew it was time to leave. (The plan was to wait the storm out in the car for 10 or 15 minutes and carry on.) Some other people were swimming, and we decided to take photos of each other for posterity's sake. We did not exchange names or anything. We did not know that a 'seek shelter immediately' warning had been issued. We just knew that the sky was coming together into something blue and green and white and black and threatening."

the house, one punctured the roof over the garage. But it doesn't take too long to realize how lucky you are. We've got a heck of a view of East Bay now."

Linda Bell lives on Skegemog Point Road, with 500 feet of frontage on Elk Lake. Three trees fell on the house, damaging her bedroom and other parts of the home, while the side lot is dotted with holes where excavators have removed root balls.

Because of the storm, her views to the south and north on Elk Lake are much better, and she's met neighbors she never knew before.

"Our minds have amazing resilience," she said. "It doesn't take long for us to change our mental image of how things have changed and to accept that as all right."

Tom Ulrich, deputy superintendent for Sleeping Bear Dunes National Lakeshore, didn't hesitate a second when asked what the storm's toll means for the park's designation in 2011 by viewers of ABC's "Good Morning America" as the most beautiful spot in the nation. "If you're standing in the middle of one of the areas most damaged you might not think that, but we're a 71,000-acre park and the vast majority was not affected," he said.

"It's still the most beautiful place in America."

The Homestead, Leelanau County
Photo by Sarah Knapp
After the storm.

Manistee, Manistee County
Photo by Walter Smart
An image of the extreme southern edge of the storm as captured by Walter Smart while on the beach at Bar Lake, just a couple miles north of Manistee. "It was slow in its travel across Lake Michigan, but upon arrival it cleared the beach with high winds and a rapid decrease in temperature."

FIRST SIGHTINGS

MANISTEE
FRANKFORT
MANITOU ISLANDS
LITTLE GLEN LAKE
LITTLE TRAVERSE LAKE
TRAVERSE CITY

Frankfort, Benzie County
Photo by Aimé Merizon

"My friend and I had a great meal and mead at Stormcloud Brewing Company, then went down to the beach to watch the surfers. Suddenly the sky grew dark and the wind picked up. We abandoned our bench, but not before rooting for the boat racing the storm for the harbor."

U.S. Coast Guard Lt. Cmdr. Charter Tschirgi wrote the following email regarding Air Station Traverse City's helicopter rescue of a 33-year-old kayaker off South Manitou Island. Tschirgi captured the scenes at right with his iPhone.

"CGC ALDER was underway when the 02AUG15 wind storm hit. [Our logs from the day] show wind speeds and lake temps we took during the storm. The logs do not reflect it, but I saw wind gusts up to 55 kts out of the north. It made for very odd lake conditions because we had a 5-foot swell out of the south being hit by 50 kt wind gusts from the north. The sustained winds were 30 kts out of the north.

"For the rescue of the missing kayaker, we searched a trackline between Southern and Northern Manitou Islands. My assumption was that the individual would be blown south by the wind. We located his kayak approximated 2–3 nautical miles SE of his last known position. Air Station Traverse City rescued the individual about 500 yds south of his water logged kayak. The gentleman had a life jacket and light with him. Both items were critical to his survival."

"I was born and raised
in Traverse City and I've never
seen anything like this.
It's astounding that no one
was killed."

George Weeks, 83,
who lives in Glen Haven

Little Glen Lake, Leelanau County
Photo by Brady Binstadt
Three minutes before the storm wind swept in over Lake
Michigan and down the Dune Climb at Sleeping Bear,
Brady Binstadt shot this photo from the backyard of his
parent's Southpointe Road home on Little Glen Lake.

Little Traverse Lake, Leelanau County
Photo by Joseph Celentino
Storm cloud front taken from the Celentino Beach over
Little Traverse Lake, Aug. 2, at 4:14 PM.

"I'm sure if this
had happened at night,
we would have had
many fatalities."

Bruce Smith, chief meteorologist,
National Weather Service,
Gaylord

●●●●○ AT&T 📶 4:51 PM 81% 🔋
accuweather.com

Weather Radar for Lake Leelanau

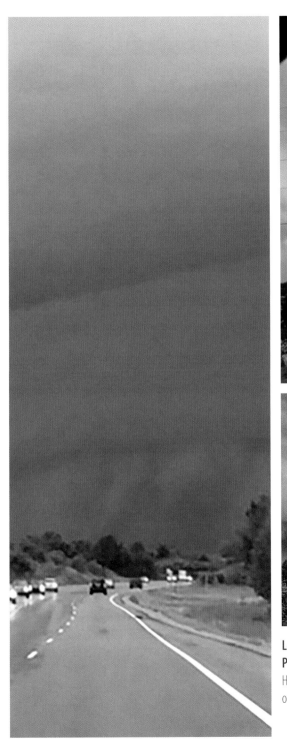

Traverse City, West Side
Photo by Josh Guldner

Leelanau County
Photos (left and top) by David Helm
Headed to Empire at around 4:35 p.m. with a kayak on the roof of his car, David Helm of Newport, Ky., pulled over and captured these images of the storm as he looked north and west from M-72.

Lake Leelanau, Leelanau County
Photo by Marcy Rogers
Preparing dinner with her sister, Marcy Rogers looked out of her cottage to see what she described as "some unusual clouds" rolling in. "I remember how calm the water was, which seemed so odd to me given the fierceness of the sky. I only managed a few photos before it was clear that I needed to take cover, as the plastic Adirondack chairs and sand buckets began blowing across the lawn."

STORM

LEELANAU COUNTY

SLEEPING BEAR DUNES

GLEN HAVEN

LELAND

LAKE LEELANAU

GLEN ARBOR

BIG & LITTLE GLEN LAKES

Stu Stu Studio ©2015

Sleeping Bear Dunes, Leelanau County
Photo by Cheri Willow Fettes

"We were eating dinner at the Western Avenue Grill when the storm hit. We watched the vertical winds blow from the south, tearing out the tree that was on the corner of the building we were in. We turned in our seats to see it better, and watched a tree tumble onto the house right across the street. We decided it would be wise to step away from all of the big windows. After finishing our meal, we went outside as soon as the rain stopped. Another tree was down, just across the driveway from our vehicle, falling again towards the north and missing us.

"We drove through flooded streets, taking each road out of Glen Arbor as far as we could go until forced back by downed trees across the roads. We noticed that the road going toward Glen Haven was not backed up with traffic, and took that around towards the Dune Climb, having to ride the shoulder many times to get around the downed trees.

"At the entrance to the Dune Climb, there were officials from the Sleeping Bear Dunes National Lakeshore directing all traffic into the parking Lot. They needed the roads clear so they could remove trees and debris from the roads.

"I was happy to see. . .people taking advantage of the opportunity to get out and enjoy the free climb, as the next wave of extreme weather was approaching from the south.

"A couple of hours later, we were allowed to leave the parking lot, but only to go south towards Empire. Except for local traffic, the roads to Glen Arbor were closed for many days."

Lake Leelanau, Leelanau County
Photo by Marcy Rogers

The storm ultimately passed as quickly as it came. Aside from a fallen tree and the loss of power, the Rogers family was safe. After dinner, they decided to drive to Glen Arbor for ice cream. "Little did we realize, there would be no ice cream that night. The town and dunes we had enjoyed only days before, were now coming to rest under the storm's steepest toll. The fireman at the road block said it best: 'Lady, the only way into Glen Arbor tonight is by boat or helicopter.'"

In the wake of the storm, some people asked, Why didn't we hear sirens? Sirens only have about a one-mile range and cost more than $50,000 apiece. In 2014, Grand Traverse County contracted with an emergency-alert provider CodeRED to allow citizens to get emergency alerts on smart phones, tablets or computers by text and/or email. The county's alert of a severe storm warning went out 45 minutes before the storm hit its border. Go to www.grandtraverse.org/CodeRED to sign up. It's recommended that citizens use a large-screen tablet, desktop or laptop for the sign-up.

Leelanau County has sirens that weren't used because there was no tornado. Matt Ansorge, Leelanau's emergency services director, said CodeRED is too expensive and the county's population has many elderly people who wouldn't use it. The county is examining other alternatives.

Lake Leelanau, off South Solon Park Road
Photo by Jeff Herman

STRUCK

Gov. Rick Snyder declared a state of emergency in Leelanau County on Aug. 10.

More than 4,200 cubic yards of logs and brush were deposited at the designated county drop site at Myles Kimmerly Park.

At the end of August, there was $23.9 million calculated in personal property damage. The population of Leelanau County is approximately 21,500.

Worst-hit areas were Alligator Hill and its base along the Heritage Trail in Sleeping Bear Dunes National Lakeshore, Dunns Farm Road and Northwood Drive.

Glen Lake, Leelanau County
Photo by Jim Anderson
Damage on the hill southwest of Glen Arbor,
looking west.

"It looked like someone just went bowling in the forest.

Everything was knocked down."

John Soderholm, supervisor, Glen Arbor Township

Photo by Tom Dumas

Northwood Drive, Glen Arbor, Leelanau County
Bridget Devlin

Three days into a northern Michigan vacation and with no idea a huge storm was brewing, Bridget Devlin had just come back from a long bike ride and was enjoying a beer on the porch of her rental cabin near Northwoods Drive when the storm hit. "Suddenly, the lights flickered and went out, the rain pelted, the wind roared and all around was the sound of trees cracking and then thumping when they hit the ground. A tree fell onto the roof of the cabin with a terrible noise, shook the place, then broke in two — the other half landed directly on my car. It was a little like the tornado scene from 'The Wizard of Oz'; trees, branches, debris were flying everywhere." For Devlin the chaos seemed to last only five minutes, but in that time she thought she was a goner. "I grew up in Traverse City and remember tornado drills and spending some time in our basement listening to the radio. But I never remember a storm of this caliber. I've lived in California for the last 40 or so years, and think that I prefer earthquakes now."

Northwood Drive, Glen Lake, Leelanau County
Photo by Tom Dumas

Summer residents and locals living on and around Northwoods Drive in Leelanau County took a direct hit from driving storm winds. When Indiana resident Tom Dumas and his family saw the sky getting progressively darker, they ran for the basement and for 20 minutes heard and felt the house shaking nonstop as trees fell outside. After the powerful winds subsided, Dumas looked outside to see seven trees fallen on his one-acre property. One hit the house. Another crushed his car. The driveway was completely covered with downed trees. And, out on the lake, the family's boat was tossed off its Shore Station, which had also been overturned by the wind. With over 44 trees scattered like matchsticks over the roadway, Northwood Drive (pictured) was completely impassable. The Dumas family was unable to leave their house for three days while crews worked to clear the driveway and the main road. Insurance estimates for the damage and tree removal were $60,000.

Glen Arbor, Leelanau County
Photo by Michele Aucello
M-109 looking towards the Dunes from the Day Forest intersection.

Glen Arbor, Leelanau County
Photo by Kyler Phillips
Impassable M-22.

TERROR AMONG THE TREES

BY ROBERT CAMPBELL

D.H Day. Photo by Tom Ulrich

D.H Day. Photo by Tom Ulrich

O ne of Tim Harbin's great joys in life is rustic camping with his wife and four daughters. And one of their favorite places is the D.H. Day Campground in the Sleeping Bear Dunes National Lakeshore.

Sunday, Aug. 2, was the fifth day at their campsite. The family had spent their week doing the things that helped Sleeping Bear Lakeshore win the designation "Most Beautiful Place in America" by viewers of *ABC's Good Morning America* in 2011.

Tim, wife, Karin, and daughters Jacquelyn, 17, Elizabeth, 16, Christina, 13, and Marilyn, 11, had walked at least one hiking trail every day, enjoyed the magical views from Sleeping Bear's hills and beaches, rode their bikes along the park's Heritage Trail into Glen Arbor for ice cream and checked out merchandise at Cherry Republic.

Harbin, a dentist in Gaylord, is a prudent man. On that Sunday, he was following radar on his smartphone. A campground host had warned campers at 10 a.m. about the possibility of 60 mph winds and golf ball-sized hail later in the day, but two waves of storms had passed without incident. The third was more worrisome.

"I'm looking at the radar on my iPhone and seeing a big orange, red, purple band."

Harbin said. "There was a little bulge, and it was heading right toward us. I collected the girls and headed back to camp."

By the time they scrambled inside their pop-up camper, the rain had started. Within minutes hundreds of acorns were pelting the camper.

"It just got louder and louder," he said. "I looked out the door and there were three trees on the ground within 20 feet of our camper. I yelled at the girls to get in the Suburban. We had to get out of there."

They drove their way around and under fallen trees until they found an open spot nearby and waited the winds out. It was immediately clear that the storm might have exacted a terrible human toll. Harbin told Karin he had to go back; he had medical training and thought he could help.

What he saw was chilling: large trees had crushed several tents. He went to each one.

"The most difficult thing was the helpless feeling I had when opening those tents."

Incredibly, no one was injured.

A young mother nursing her baby realized just in time she had to get out. Seconds later, she turned to watch a tree crush her tent. At another campsite, a family of four was huddled in their pop-up when a tree smashed one end of the camper, barely missing them.

D.H. Day. Photo by Tim Harbin

Harbin returned to his family and other stranded campers—no one could leave because trees blocked all the roads. They were tired and hungry and Harbin decided to cook dinner over an open fire.

"I usually try to keep calm and focus on how I can keep my family safe. But that night I kept wondering if there still might be someone in the campground."

Campers had filled all 88 of the rustic sites on Aug. 2, said Tom Ulrich, Sleeping Bear's deputy superintendent. None suffered serious injury.

"Just," said Ulrich, "incredible luck."

D.H. Day. Photo by Tim Harbin

Glen Haven, Sleeping Bear Dunes, Leelanau County
Photo by Shannon Rogers

"If you're standing in the middle of one of the areas most damaged you might not think it, but we're a 71,000-acre park and the vast majority was not affected. It's still the most beautiful place in America."

Tom Ulrich, deputy superintendent, Sleeping Bear Dunes National Lakeshore.
In 2011, *ABC's Good Morning America* viewers voted the park the most beautiful spot in the nation.

**Glen Haven, Sleeping Bear Dunes,
Leelanau County
Photos by Tom Ulrich**

Damage in and around the Sleeping Bear Dunes was so terrible in places that it rendered some areas unrecognizable. Around Glen Haven and the popular D.H. Day Campground, crews worked for two weeks to get the campground back up and running on Aug. 16.

Photo by Kyler Phillips
A park sign that points to downed trees instead of the Heritage Trail.

Photo by Friends of the Sleeping Bear Dunes

FRIENDS CLEAR THE WAY

BY ROBERT CAMPBELL

Before Sunday services at the First Church of Christ, Scientist in Glen Arbor, Jim Munson often can be found clearing leaves from the parking lot with his power blower. Just down the road from the church is the entrance to the section of the Sleeping Bear Heritage Trail that connects the busy resort village with Glen Haven.

Until the Aug. 2 windstorm, that part of the trail was notable for the feel it gave hikers and bicyclists of slipping through a cool, heavily shaded tunnel of trees.

Later, when Munson took his first look after the storm, "I was sad," he said. "There are several areas that just took my breath away."

Over a mile and a half of the paved trail fell victim to the 90-100 mph winds, exposing a former forest that in the aftermath more closely resembled a landscape of giant broken toothpicks.

Said Leonard Marszalek, who manages the trail for the nonprofit Friends of Sleeping Bear Dunes: "It's like Montana. It's all Big Sky. It looks kind of like a volcano exploded. I won't see it like it was again in my lifetime."

But Marszalek and Kerry Kelly, chairman of the Friends of Sleeping Bear Dunes, didn't have much time to pout about what had been. Their group is responsible for much of the maintenance of the trail under an agreement with the National Park Service. The day after the storm, their board convened and put out a

Photo by Bob Campbell

43

call for help. That Tuesday, eight volunteers joined them. By Friday, there were 52.

They removed limbs, branches and debris from trees blocking about 8 miles of the trail — a few of the volunteers were certified to use chainsaws on national park land. In total 138 volunteers — 85 new to the group — worked more than 1,000 hours over six days with chainsaws, loppers and handsaws, and hauling brush. When they finished, a park service team came in with bigger saws to finish the job and reopen the trail to walkers and riders.

As of mid-summer 2015, the Heritage Trail was 17.5 miles long with plans to add another 10 miles over the next few years. For bike riders, it has become a destination offering the unusual combination of pavement, curves and hills. Most paved trails are on abandoned railroad tracks and are relatively straight with only slight elevation changes.

Except for the hardest hit stretch between the two towns, people who don't realize there was a storm won't notice, Kelly said.

For him, it was the team effort that was most gratifying. "The community really responded," he said.

Photos (above and bottom right) by Friends of Sleeping Bear Dunes

Photo by U.S. Coast Guard

Photo by Beth Hobbes Chiles

Hundreds of trees went down on the Sleeping Bear Heritage Trail

from Empire to Port Oneida.

One hundred thirty-eight Friends of Sleeping Bear Dunes volunteers

logged 1,053 hours after the storm to get the trail back open.

The storm left some people in rural areas without power for as many as five days. FEMA recommends a three-day emergency supply of water and food in households. Leelanau County Sheriff Mike Borkovich said a 30-day supply is needed. Grand Traverse County suggests seven days.

"It's like Montana. It's all Big Sky now."

Leonard Marszalek, manager of Friends of Sleeping Bear Dunes, the volunteer group that maintains the park's biking and hiking trail, referring to the storm-changed view from parts of the trail.

(Left) Leelenau Trail, Leelanau County
Before the clean-up.
Photo by Friends of Sleeping Bear Dunes

(This page) Leelanau Trail, Leelanau County
After the clean-up.
Photo by Friends of Sleeping Bear Dunes

47

"It sounded like a train
coming down the street."

David Thomasma,
owner of Synchronocity,
an art gallery in Glen Arbor

Glen Arbor, Leelanau County
Photos (left and right) by Donna Kaplowitz
M-22 was open for pedestrians for a brief time the morning
after the storm. Then the electrical crews came in and
closed it to all — access to Glen Arbor was only by boat or by beach.

Glen Arbor, Leelanau County
Photo by Annie Rollo
Western Avenue Grill on Western Avenue in downtown Glen Arbor.

Glen Arbor, Leelanau County
Photo by JoAnna and Bob Rodgers
Uprooted trees crushed the porch and an outdoor shed at the home of Glen Arbor's Bob and JoAnna Rodgers.

Glen Arbor, Leelanau County
Photo by Kevin Wolma

Leelanau County
Photo by Michele Aucello
The yard of the Manor On Glen Lake, south of Little Glen, minus the willow and cottonwood trees.

Glen Arbor, Leelanau County
Photo by Annie Rollo
Annie Rollo took a walk around downtown Glen Arbor after the storm and captured this image of the giant red oak that fell on the Serbin Real Estate Building, on the corner of Western Avenue and South Oak Street. While it did not penetrate the building, the massive tree pushed the building 3 feet off its foundation and destroyed the interior.

Glen Arbor,
Leelanau County
Photo by Kyler Phillips
A pine uprooted and leaning against a house on the corner of M-22 and Pine Street.

Little Glen Lake,
Leelanau County
Photo by Elizabeth Bartlett
In the 60 years her family has owned property on the western shore of Little Glen Lake — right across the street from the Sleeping Bear Dunes National Lakeshore — Elizabeth Bartlett never remembered seeing the lake level drop as dramatically as it did during the windy peak of the storm.

For about 30 minutes, all the water in the lake seemed to have been "pushed" eastward — roughly a two-foot drop — exposing the lake's sandy bottom. "It took about 30 minutes for the lake levels to return to normal. When the storm was over, the water came back — first rising over the top of the neighbor's dock, a foot or more above average — before quickly leveling out."

Glen Arbor, Leelanau County
Photos by Kyler Phillips
The canoe portage on Crystal View Road blocked
by large trees.

Power lines sliced through a road sign along M-22
towards Port Oneida.

Glen Arbor, Leelanau County
Photo by Donna Kaplowitz
M-22 between the bridge and Leelanau School at Overbrook Road, an hour after the storm.

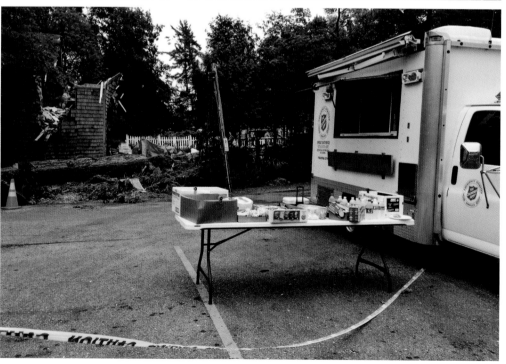

Glen Arbor, Leelanau County
Photo by Ruth Blick
The Director of Development for The Salvation Army, Ruth Blick, shot this photo behind the Glen Arbor Township building while Emergency Disaster Services was providing lunches to volunteers from the Southern Baptist Disaster Relief Team.

Glen Lake, Leelanau County
Photo by Stacy Knutson

Damage outside the summer home of Stacy Knutson, whose family has vacationed in Glen Arbor every summer for the last 87 years.

Glen Lake, Leelanau County
(above) Photo by Toby West

The storm downed three large trees in the center of Villa Glen Cottages, a lakeside rental property located on Big Glen Lake across from Alligator Hill. One of the trees fell on the cottage occupied by Toby West and his family.

Photo by Donna Kaplowitz

White Pine Trail, Glen Arbor, Leelanau County
Photo (left) by JoAnna and Bob Rodgers
Nature vs. landscaping.

Little Glen Lake, Leelanau County
Photo (center) by Tom Ricketts
Tom Ricketts and his family left their vacation home on Little Glen well ahead of the storm, only to get a call later that night from neighbors who said trees were down, power was out and the family's boat dock had been flipped over during the storm. "After seeing some images from Facebook and the news, I knew it was bad. I felt bad that our neighbors were there without power. So I loaded up my generator and called my Uncle Tony and a buddy Jeff, who had some heavy duty chainsaws. We packed water and plenty of gas and spent the next day helping clear paths and moving tree debris. We ended the day with a dip in Glen Lake and a ride into town to see the damage and have a beer at Art's Tavern. After a day of tasting sawdust, the taste of a cold Bell's Oberon was a welcome relief."

Glen Arbor, Leelanau County
Photo (top, right) by Michele Aucello
Across from Myles Kimmerly Park in Kasson Township, three days after the storm, tree removal crews took a break for dinner before returning to work.

Glen Arbor, Leelanau County
Photo (center, right) by Tim Harbin
D-H Day clean-up.

Glen Arbor, Leelanau County
Photo (bottom, right) by Nancy Temple
The sign says "Open," but, as electric crews and volunteers worked to clear roads and repair downed power lines, the town of Glen Arbor was essentially closed in the days after the storm.

The Homestead, Glen Arbor
Photo by Mark Husnick
Bay Mountain, just before the storm.

The bride and groom, Katie Yazvac and Kirk Johnson.

Photo by Tom Yazvac

A WEDDING SURVIVES THE STORM

BY ROBERT CAMPBELL

Photo by Mark Husnick

Katie Yazvac wanted the perfect venue for her marriage to Kirk Johnson — atop a hill overlooking Lake Michigan. She found it at Bay Mountain, the highest ski hill at the Homestead Resort just north of Glen Arbor.

A week before the Aug. 2 ceremony, the weather reports looked good. And then they didn't. Still, said Katie: "I was certain those storms wouldn't happen on my wedding day." Watching radar on their phones and tablets, they felt confident the storm wouldn't hit land until 5 p.m.

The wedding was to begin around 4:30, so they moved it up 10 minutes. But Kirk had misplaced his vows and there was a late search for missing bridesmaid flowers.

"That's the only reason I didn't get soaked," said Katie, a veterinarian from Cascade, near Grand Rapids, who was waiting with her bridesmaids and her father at the bottom of the hill. Even with the first thunderclaps, she thought they could pull it off. Her confidence faded as she watched about 50 wedding guests, led by her fleet-footed cousins, come running down the hill. "I'll never forget that sight."

After taking refuge briefly in the golf pro shop, the wedding party hustled to Mountain Flowers Lodge for the reception but soon descended to the flooding basement because of tornado warnings. After the last of the storm passed, they moved upstairs, set up a makeshift altar and, by candle and window light, the couple read their vows. With electricity out, the musician hired to play piano keyboards was stranded in a shed at the top of the mountain.

Undeterred, a groomsman raced to get a Bluetooth wireless speaker from his car, and Katie's dad, Tom, downloaded the processional, the "Warsaw Concerto," onto his iPhone. Later, Dad whistled the recessional, "The Sailor's Hornpipe."

An obliging Homestead staff then shuttled the group to its Camp Firefly lodge for the reception. Kirk, a veterinarian specializing in care of horses, called a client in Traverse City and asked if he had a generator. He did and, amazingly, Kirk's cousin Josh drove to town and back — finding the rare roads not blocked by trees. By the time dinner ended, the party was ready to rock. With power, a DJ got the party back in business.

"We danced until 11 o'clock," said the mother of the bride.

Photo by Rean Bush

Old Mission Peninsula, Grand Traverse County
Photo by Barbara Weber
When Barbara Weber stopped to take these photos between the Bayside and Quaker Valley neighborhoods on Old Mission Peninsula, she could see lightning bolts in the distance, behind the wall of clouds, over the Leelanau Peninsula. Then everything turned bright green. "It was breathtaking and beautiful and ominous and a little scary all at the same time."

STORM
TRAVERSE CITY
& OLD MISSION PENINSULA

Old Mission Peninsula, Grand Traverse County
Photo by Barbara Weber

Elmwood Township Marina, Grand Traverse County
Photos by Eric Currin

63

"We counted 16 root balls, two trees on the house; one punctured the roof over the garage. But it doesn't take too long to realize how lucky you are. We've got a heck of a view of East Bay now."

Bill Stott, who lives with his wife, Robbin, in a development along Bluff Road in Peninsula Township

Traverse City, Grand Traverse County
Photos by Mark Preseau

Looking like a column from a nuclear blast, the shelf cloud moved fast over the subdivision where Mark Preseau took these pictures from his deck. "I have lived in northern Michigan most of my life and I have never seen anything like this. I was so impressed with the cloud formation and how unusual it was. I acted quickly to snap a few pictures because the storm passed over my house in a matter of minutes."

Neahtawanta, Grand Traverse County
Photo by Jaime Al-Shamma

65

Old Mission Peninsula,
Grand Traverse County
Photo by Heidi Brown
Coming south down Old Mission Peninsula, Heidi Brown was headed to work with a friend when they saw the approaching storm cloud and stopped to take a picture.

Traverse City, Grand Traverse County
Photos by Justin Perry
Right before everything went "all Armageddon," Justin Perry had just finished up at The Workshop
playing a gig with his band, G-Snacks. He left the brew pub and captured the left-hand image over
West Bay near the volleyball courts, just west of the Open Space.

"I was hunched over and I said, 'OK, God, you know what, you got me here for a reason and now you've got my attention.' I told him I was a pretty darned good person and you've got to take care of me now."

Carol Vernam, 57, who was headed to her home on Old Mission Peninsula when a tree crushed her '05 Volkswagen Beetle convertible, leaving her pinned inside. (See page 78.)

Traverse City, Grand Traverse County
Photo by Natalie Beebe

A look at shoppers racing to their cars ahead of the storm cloud moving over Oleson's grocery store off at the corner of Three Mile and Hammond roads. Meteorologists who contacted Natalie Beebe after her photo went viral on the internet attributed the green and blue color of the storm cloud to hail trapped inside of a cloud. The icy pellets of frozen rain reflected sunlight, creating the amazing colors and glow.

Traverse City, Grand Traverse County
Photos by T Mair

Photographer T Mair wrote this about the photos above taken on Front Street:

"The lighter colored clouds are the head, or beginning, and if you have seen other storm cloud photos from that time (approx 4:30) this one only shows a partial view of what looked like a dome shaped cloud. No rain yet. Upper cloud moving at high speed.

"The second and darker photo is seconds before the rain and wind come. Wind comes/ moves down to ground. Notice dark mini funnel forming.

"The TCFF banner across Front Street comes down or actually unstretches and wads up on the line it is attached to. Everyone outdoors then runs for cover. Surprisingly no planters blow/fall off utility lights and no letters blow off The State marquee."

BULLETIN - IMMEDIATE BROADCAST REQUESTED
SEVERE THUNDERSTORM WARNING
NATIONAL WEATHER SERVICE GAYLORD MI
357 PM EDT SUN AUG 2 2015

THE NATIONAL WEATHER SERVICE IN GAYLORD HAS ISSUED A

* SEVERE THUNDERSTORM WARNING FOR...
BENZIE COUNTY IN NORTHERN MICHIGAN...
WEXFORD COUNTY IN NORTHERN MICHIGAN...
GRAND TRAVERSE COUNTY IN NORTHERN MICHIGAN...
MANISTEE COUNTY IN NORTHERN MICHIGAN...
LEELANAU COUNTY IN NORTHERN MICHIGAN...

* UNTIL 500 PM EDT
* AT 356 PM EDT...SEVERE THUNDERSTORMS WERE LOCATED ALONG A LINE EXTENDING FROM 18 MILES NORTHWEST OF SLEEPING BEAR POINT TO 20 MILES EAST OF ALGOMA...MOVING SOUTHEAST AT 45 MPH.

HAZARD...70 MPH WIND GUSTS AND PENNY SIZE HAIL.

SOURCE...RADAR INDICATED.

IMPACT...EXPECT CONSIDERABLE TREE DAMAGE. DAMAGE IS LIKELY TO MOBILE HOMES...ROOFS AND OUTBUILDINGS.

* LOCATIONS IMPACTED INCLUDE...
TRAVERSE CITY...CADILLAC...MANISTEE...ELK RAPIDS...THOMPSONVILLE... EMPIRE...BEULAH...SLEEPING BEAR POINT...BINGHAM...KINGSLEY... MANTON...SHERMAN...GLEN ARBOR...BUCKLEY...BOON...SUTTONS BAY... NORTHPORT...EASTLAKE...BENZONIA AND KALEVA.

PRECAUTIONARY/PREPAREDNESS ACTIONS...

FOR YOUR PROTECTION MOVE TO AN INTERIOR ROOM ON THE LOWEST FLOOR OF A BUILDING.

TORNADO...POSSIBLE
HAIL...0.75IN
WIND...70MPH

Carol Tompkins-Parker

"I was concessions manager during TC Film Fest at Lars Hockstad. I was doing an inventory count when I noticed the strong winds outside. Looking out the closed blinds in the large classroom fronting West Eighth, I saw the trees were bending in half due to the winds....and the sky was green! I know that green skies mean strong possibility of tornado.

"I quickly left the room and ran down the hall to the West Seventh Street main entrance to Lars. I was stunned, watching the radar on the Weather Channel, and found Film Fest co-founder John Robert Williams was also checking the intense, fast moving storm on another weather website on his phone.

"Two TCAPS maintenance men were also at the Seventh Street foyer, stating that all the movie goers were in the safest place in all the school building.

"We ushered every volunteer looking at the storm and falling trees away from the doors into the hallway. A nurse ran in from the pouring rains. She had blood to deliver to Munson ER but could not proceed any further due to large trees down, blocking the street. She soon left, driving in reverse on Seventh Street, and hopefully got to Munson safe.

"The Film Fest patrons at the conclusion of the 3 p.m. show were informed there had been a storm whilst they were enjoying the movie. Two vehicles were damaged by falling trees.

"Meanwhile, folks braved the weather to see the 6 p.m. show. The handicapped and elderly patrons sat on chairs we provided in the hallway. The more able-bodied walked into the large gym and were seated on the bleachers upstairs until we admitted them to the auditorium."

Traverse City, Boardman Street
Photo by Jocelyn Trepte
Ken and Joan Richmond's historic Boardman neighborhood home was built in the early 1870s. The trees — silver maple and giant catalpa — were likely planted at the same time.

STRUCK

Grand Traverse County's storm toll is estimated at $15.2 million.

Grand Traverse County ranks third among Michigan's 83 counties for leisure travel, with an estimated annual spending of $924.5 million.

Traverse City area towing services responded to more than 100 calls for storm damaged vehicles.

The worst hit areas in Grand Traverse County were along the shorelines of East Bay and West Bay on the southern half of Old Mission Peninsula, Traverse City north of 14th Street, along the East Bay shorefront to Yuba, inland to the orchards south of Elk Rapids and along Elk and Skegemog lakes.

Traverse City, Washington Street
Photos by Carol Tompkins-Parker

"The morning after the storm, I was riding my bike across town to check on some friends on East State Street. The house is located on the 800 block of Washington Street; it's difficult to read the address for obvious reasons. This tree had split, crashing between two houses, half of the tree landing on its front porch. It was also totally uprooted from the front yard.

"Due to fallen trees throughout town, some alleys were impassable. This lovely tree (left) is half-dangling onto the power lines. This was located at the alley between West Sixth and Seventh Streets, the 300 block, facing west. The tree was a power outage source for the south side of the street."

"I believe this is going to be the costliest storm
in the history of the county."

Gregg Bird, emergency management coordinator
for Grand Traverse County

Traverse City, Chippewa Street
Photo by Carol Anderson

Three huge trees crashed onto the roof of Carol Anderson's home. During the worst of the storm, Anderson was only concerned for the welfare of her cat, Mitchell. Not knowing if the animal was inside or had somehow gotten out, Anderson was frantically searching room-to-room in the home "as destruction ruled outdoors." She eventually found the animal curled up behind the water heater, safe and sound.

A SMASHED BEETLE; SHE WALKS AWAY

BY ROBERT CAMPBELL

Carol Vernam had just finished shopping at Cali's women's clothing store in downtown Traverse City when the rain began. She was eager to get home, about 6 miles up Old Mission Peninsula, where her husband, Lance, was barbequing ribs to go with farm stand sweet corn.

Vernam, 57, a saleswoman for Bill Marsh Auto Group in Traverse City, was driving her pride-and-joy summer car — a Cobalt Blue '05 Volkswagen Beetle convertible with a turbo engine. The top was up, a Dave Matthews CD was playing on her stereo, and Carol was rolling with energy as she headed north up Peninsula Drive toward Eastern Avenue.

Suddenly, the wind picked up, the sky darkened and a large limb fell across the road in front of her. She quickly decided to take the longer route home along East Bay. She turned around in a driveway, began to accelerate and immediately heard a CRACK! Then BOOM! A huge tree slammed across the car's top, pushed Carol's headrest and seat forward, crushed her dashboard and pinned her inside. The VW, still in gear, was stopped in its tracks.

"The noise was unbelievable. All I could see was the huge trunk. The music was still playing. It was all pretty surreal."

Carol decided it was time to talk to God.

"I was hunched over and I said, 'OK, God, you know what, you got me here for a reason, and now you've got my attention.' I told him I was a pretty darned good person and you've got to take care of me now. I've done good work, and I've got a lot more good work to do."

Dave Matthews was still singing when she heard a voice asking, "Are you OK?"

The man had already called 911, but said he would try to get her out of the car. She warned him to be careful of downed power lines. He said he was assured the lines were dead.

Two others joined him to free her, with one pushing down hard on her seat cushion, creating just enough of a gap to extract her from the car. A few minutes later, Lance arrived and they headed home. "I was silent all the way. I put my head between my knees and just wept, realizing how blessed I was."

Back home, the power was out, but their home wasn't damaged. Neighbors joined them for a candlelight dinner, and she recounted her near-death experience.

"I loved that car, but I love my life better."

**Traverse City, Grand Traverse County
Photo by Carol Vernam**

**Old Mission Peninsula,
Grand Traverse County
Photo by Heidi Brown**
When the storm hit land, the driving rain and wind forced Heidi and her friend to pull over — just a second before a tree fell across the road in front of their car. Terrified, she tried calling her father and, over the noise outside, could barely hear him yelling for his daughter to take shelter in the nearest house. The storm passed as quickly as it came, but finding the road blocked by fallen trees and power lines, Heidi and her friend abandoned the car and walked most of the way home.

**Traverse City, Eastern Avenue
Photo by Don Nowka**
Power was out in the Orchard Heights area for four days following the storm.

East Bay, Grand Traverse County
Photo by Steve Engle
A view of the enormous shelf cloud from the vantage
point of Deepwater Point in Acme Township.

STORM ⚡

POINTS EAST

ACME

WILLIAMSBURG

ELK RAPIDS

BASS LAKE

ALDEN

SKEGEMOG POINT

Williamsburg, Grand Traverse County
Photo by Caitlin Scroggins

"It looked like a tidal wave coming," recalled 18-year-old Caitlin Scroggins. "The sky got dark and you could see the storm cloud coming, moving closer and closer every second."

Elk Rapids, Antrim County
Photo by Shawn Kellogg

Shawn Kellogg Photography

Acme, Grand Traverse County
Photo by Kristin Hussey
Driving into Acme along M-72 and seeing the approaching storm, Kristin Hussey and her husband pulled into the parking lot of Turtle Creek Casino. Violent wind and rain struck seconds after this photo.

Bass Lake, Elk Rapids, Antrim County
Photos by Kathy Bryant and Judy Morgan

Summering in her fifth-wheel trailer at the Honcho Rest Campground on Bass Lake in Antrim County, Kathy Bryant and her friend Judy Morgan watched as the storm cloud rolled in over the lake. "It turned the water teal green — the same color as the sky. And then the wind started blowing and the hail began to fall. It felt like the trailer was going to come right off the ground. And the hail — after it was over, you could have gone outside and made a million snowballs."

Alden, Antrim County
Photos by Troy Molby

Unlike ocean-driven hurricanes, Great Lakes storms never get named. Troy Molby of Bellaire would like to change that. He named the storm "Leo" after capturing this storm image —a photo he called "The Lion Over Alden." Do you see it? The lion is in the center of the right-hand photo with his head to the right and tail to the left.

Fairmont Drive, north shore of Skegemog Lake, Antrim County
Photo by U.S. Coast Guard

STRUCK

Skegemog Point Road, the address of dozens of residents who live on Elk Lake and Skegemog Lake, was the worst hit spot in Grand Traverse County, officials said.

Orchards in Whitewater Township and nearby townships were wind blown, but the storm's worst sting was hail damage to apples and pears. Many of the fruits were too badly bruised to be sold.

Kalkaska County along Crystal Beach Road at the south end of Torch Lake had widespread damage. More than 100 trees in a pine plantation along Rapid City Road were left in an odd and uniform distortion, tilting toward the southeast.

Skegemog Lake, Antirm County
Photos by Richard Murrell
Seeing cars like this make it all the more remarkable that no one was killed.

Fairmont Drive on the north shore of Lake Skegemog was even harder hit
than Crystal Beach. Very little was spared along the entire shoreline.

STORM UNITES
A NEIGHBORHOOD
BY ROBERT CAMPBELL

Three families — the Claudepierres, the McClinticks and the Werners — live on quiet Fairmont Drive on the north shore of Skegemog Lake in Antrim County. They have been friends since they built their homes there in the 1980s. Over the years, they've shared dock installation duties, raft building and family stories.

After the Aug. 2 storm hit, they shared breakfast, dinner and the Werners' power generator, along with the hard work of clearing each other's driveways and properties of fallen trees, for five consecutive days.

The story of their fellowship and shared approach to cleanup was not uncommon across the breadth of the storm's track. What was remarkable, though, was that they were recovering in relative obscurity, compared to the better known storm targets of Glen Arbor, the Old Mission Peninsula and Skegemog Point Road.

Dale and Gini Claudepierre were at a dinner party on Elk Lake when the storm struck and realized they needed to get home fast. Roads were blocked and they had to snake their way down an open two-track farm lane to reach Fairmont.

Bruce McClintick was at home where a large tree fell on his roof (his wife, Carol, was at their year-round home in Midland). Karlene Werner, a widow, was home with her two adult children, their spouses and four grandchildren.

Because the Claudepierres had the only working stove — it was gas, not electric — their home became the meet-up spot for hearty breakfasts.

"Even a poorly made cup of coffee can taste great when it's the only option," said Gini. "All three families combined their breakfast foods and for five days we fed 12 to 15 people."

Other neighbors working to bring their homes back to a semblance of normalcy heard about the feasts and joined in, bringing their own contributions. Afterwards, they grabbed chainsaws, and with willing hands and strong spirits, delved into the chaos of downed trees. Even the grandkids chipped in, gathering twigs and filling the firepit under adult supervision.

At suppertime, the Werners' home emerged as the destination, and the neighbors enjoyed smoked turkey, ribs and brisket on the grill and smoker — and other fare suitable for their new lumberjack lifestyles. *(continued)*

Photo by Richard Murrell

On the Wednesday after the storm, the three neighbors took a break from the trees and booked a charter boat on East Bay. They brought home enough lake trout to make a tasty dinner.

The helping-hands theme continued through the week on Fairmont. John Peale, owner of nearby Torch River Marine, drove over a large forklift to help move some of the heaviest tree trunks. Troy McLeish, who lives on Mountain Road off Fairmont, also helped with heavy equipment. Bruce and Vickie Jacobs, who own the farm with the two-track the Claudepierres used to get home on storm Sunday, stopped by to tell the group they could use the pathway anytime it was necessary.

"It was not an event we would ever want to see repeated, but we all agreed that the fellowship we experienced working and eating together was memorable," Gini said.

Photo by Bill Weltyk (before)

Photo by Bill Weltyk (after)

Skegemog Lake, Antrim County
Photo by Bill Weltyk

Bill Weltyk estimated that well over 100 trees fell in under 15 minutes around his summer home on Fairmont Drive, along the northern shore of Lake Skegemog. At least four crashed into his house and one on the garage. Standing in front of the picture window with his wife, Weltyk didn't see the storm cloud approaching or the green sky witnessed by others in the region. "I only saw what looked like a dense fog moving across Elk Lake. Then we heard a tree fall. Then we saw another fall. And another. And another. It was unreal. And we weren't scared. Just numb. We couldn't believe it was happening. We were in a fog of falling trees."

95

Skegemog Point, Grand Traverse County
Photo by Amy Peterson
Fallen trees tore through the roof of Lorraine Casey's Elk Lake home on Skegemog Point Road.

Skegemog Point, Grand Traverse County
Photo by Bob Campbell
Mark Taylor stands beside the root ball of a fallen tree behind the Elk Lake waterfront home he and his wife, Maria, own on Skegemog Point Road. The storm dropped dozens of trees on the Taylor's eight wooded acres, blocking access to the maze of snowmobile and four-wheeler trails he's created over the years.

Photo by U.S. Coast Guard
Damage on Skegemog Lake.

Cari MacGregor-Jacob, daughter of Tom and Lois MacGregor of Elk Rapids, submitted these photos and an emailed recollection of a harrowing vacation.

It was on Sunday, August 2, just after Kalkaska, that my full-sized van surged through the storm until we couldn't see the road any more. After a tornado-like wind gust that threatened to tip my van over, we pulled off to the side of the road. My son and I stuffed our pillows up against the windshield and hoped the pea-sized hail would not bust through. Large "thunks" hit the top of the van. My husband was travelling behind me with our other son. They could not see the force of the winds like we could from the van. Eventually it passed with no noticeable damage to our vehicles. That was the start of our vacation Up North!

After following a long line of traffic up M-72, and hesitantly passing through non working red lights and railroad tracks with the warning lights blaring, we continued on our journey to find out how Grandma and Grampa had made it through the storm. One section of US31 had downed lines and we crept under like the rest of the traffic. One at a time! It looked like a green snow storm all over the road, leaves and branches covered the blacktop, giving it a surreal look.

My parents responded to our cell phone calls, sounded all right, and said a few trees were down in the driveway. I thought to myself, "Well I've got my 3 sons coming up and we can all just move the trees over and that will be that". Dad had underrated the damage. We almost drove past their house. I recognized the mailbox and pulled onto the grass. Their house could not be seen from the road, like usual, and we panicked, for sure they were squashed in their home! No, they were only trapped in their home as a large group of trees had dropped across their driveway like pick-up sticks. We found a path through the maze and there they were, happy to see us.

They never saw the trees going down. Dad was in charge of watching the bayside of the house and mom was watching the driveway. Their metal roof thundering from all the hail, making it impossible for them to hear anything else. A neighbor reported that after the storm they ran through the maze to find mom standing in the driveway with tears streaming down her face. Almost all of their giant, majestic shade trees had toppled down and a large tree had crushed a corner of the pole barn, missing Dad's Model T by 3 feet! My dad's beloved Model T was unable to get out of the pole barn to join in the upcoming Harbor Days Parade. My family enters Elk Rapids Harbor Days Parade every year with the Model T and it's the highlight of our vacation week.

My sister, Bonni, and her husband arrived with their daughter, and a lot of machinery. A tractor, a dump truck and plenty of chainsaws. Despite the power outage, we started fresh the next day with all our family — all 11 of us! The volunteer fire department saved the day with some of their members. Dave and Stefanie, their son, Andrew, and their son's friends, Dillon and Haley, came and helped us to get the Model T out! They worked tirelessly all day and cleared the driveway.

It became an endless buzz of chainsaws, humid heat from the sun and miles of walking brush to the front of the yard. The pile reached over the maximum height for pick up and we still had more to add. Logs started piling up and we started counting the fallen trees. We attempted a running count and kept getting confused, "Was it 14 or 16 trees?" I finally grabbed a black spray can and numbered all the stumps. There were 22+ trees down. (Some had crossed the neighbors property line and we weren't sure about counting them! So we just added a plus to the total.) Many were 70 years or older, by a ring count. It took 4 solid days of heavy cutting and clearing, with the following weekend for stump grinding, to make the yard look passable.

The cleanup continues with a confusing parade of insurance estimators and tree and stump-removal bidders. We probably, as a family, figured we had saved our parents $12,000 to $15,000 of costs related to the cleanup. So my old saying, "In times of need, family does the deed!" definitely comes to mind.

P.S. My oldest son, Cody, was caught with his girlfriend and friends on the Lake Michigan side of the Sleeping Bear dunes at the start of the storm and told a horrifying tale of climbing back up the hill. When the storm hit, he said all the people on that side started climbing up the hill like crabs. There were families with small children trying to get back to safety. The rain pelted them, with hail hitting their heads and backs as they struggled to make it back up the steep dune. People were screaming, "We're gonna die!" He said it took them an hour to make it up, with the one out-of-shape friend dragging behind.

Cari MacGregor-Jacob
No#1 daughter of: Tom & Lois MacGregor, Elk Rapids, Michigan

TREEMAGEDDON

Our friends the photographers sent in a variety of photos, but none more plentiful than downed trees. For many, the fallen giants meant emotional pain and days of hard work to clear the mess. But many folks also marked the historic event with poses that included children, pets and lots of root balls.

(Above) Skegemog Point
Photos by Penni Newlun and Bob Campbell
Over the years, dozens of weddings—including one the day before the storm—have been held under this perfectly shaped oak tree at the Samels Family Heritage Society's Centennial Farm on Skegemog Point Road.

(Left) Little Glen Lake, Leelanau County
Photo by Tom Ricketts

Photo by Sondra Shaw Hardy

Photo by Barbara Lockrey

Photo by Michele Aucello

Photo by Sara Knapp

(Above) Glen Lake, Leelanau County
Photo by Jessica Hoedeman

This huge maple, nearly three feet in diameter and located near Miller Hill Road in Leelanau County, looked to Jessica Hoedeman like it had been almost completely gutted.
"It's tricky to describe, but what was left inside had literally been turned into a corrugated cardboard-type material. It was like the storm had ripped out all the insides then put some back in."

Photo by Toby West

Photo by Tyler

WHEN DISASTER HITS, HEROES

BY ROBERT CAMPBELL

erriam Webster defines hero as "a person who is admired for great or brave acts or fine qualities."

In the aftermath of 2015's monumentally destructive storm, hundreds of people have stepped in to help in ways beyond what might be expected.

On Skegemog Point Road in Whitewater Township, Mike Norton, well-known to residents of the peninsula separating Elk and Skegemog lakes as a wood cutter and lot clearer, was on the road with his chainsaw — along with several others — within minutes of the storm's passage. They were clearing the many mature trees blocking the road so residents and emergency vehicles could get in and out.

The all-night scene played out across the storm-ravaged area. Leelanau County Sheriff Mike Borkovich said he couldn't count the number of people who stopped at roadblocks, where downed trees and power lines posed a threat, and asked how they could help. Soon, men with chainsaws were cutting and women and children were dragging cut branches and debris off roads.

Not all the help came from northwestern Michigan communities. A national group called the Southern Baptist Disaster Relief, which brings trained volunteers to natural disasters where residents are overwhelmed, sent 12 people with chainsaws for several days to help residents of Glen Arbor Township clear driveways and personal property of trees. The Ball Foundation (whose company roots in canning jars have moved on to recyclable metal containers) donated $10,000 through TART for Sleeping Bear Heritage Trail restoration.

And how about Randy Chamberlain, chef and owner of the upscale restaurant Blu in Glen Arbor, who donated 100 duck confit dinners for people stranded in the village and staying at the township hall until roads could be cleared. Talk about bon appétit! He repeated the gesture with a free lunch later in the week. Glen Arborites also enjoyed meals supplied by the Red Cross and Salvation Army.

A shout out to those who rose to the challenge would be incomplete without mentioning the hundreds of police, firefighters, utility workers, park officials and U.S. Coast Guard men and women called upon to work long hours — in some cases for many days — under trying circumstances. We'll highlight Petty Officer 3rd Class Nickolaus Trimpe, the rescue swimmer who helped a 33-year-old man who spent nearly six hours in the water near South Manitou Island after his kayak was swamped. Trimpe helped the man into a basket lowered from a Coast Guard helicopter based in Traverse City. The Leelanau County Sheriff Marine Patrol and Coast Guard boats from Frankfort and Duluth also played key roles in the rescue. Kudos, too, to firefighters from Northport, Suttons Bay and Leland for helping their comrades in Glen Lake Township, going door-to-door to every one of 2,300 homes to make sure no one needed assistance.

Sheriff Borkovich and his command team issued a letter of commendation to his patrol, marine and corrections divisions for their roles. "You were asked and stepped up to work long hours and extra shifts, often in hazardous areas with power lines and trees down," the commendation said. The sheriff also noted that many brought their personal chainsaws to scenes to help clear roads.

In time of crisis, an informed citizenry is critical. If you live near Glen Arbor, the epicenter of the storm's first strike, consider yourself lucky to have had the *Glen Arbor Sun*, its editor Jacob Wheeler and a thin but capable staff delivering helpful, insightful and well-written reports online and in print editions.

ARE MADE

In neighborhoods, individuals contributed in small but important ways. On Skegemog Point, resident Bonnie Hector worked with the Village Market in Central Lake to donate bottled water, candles and batteries for residents without water and power.

Politicians often are the subject of scorn — sometimes deservedly. But a crisis reveals those elected officials who are true public servants. Whitewater Township Supervisor Ron Popp wasn't just managing his township's response to the emergency, for 12 hours a day for more than a week; he was at the controls of a front-end loader loaned by a Kalkaska excavator to compact a debris drop-off site on Skegemog Point Road. In Glen Arbor Township, supervisor John Soderholm, trapped by trees over his own driveway the first day, tipped his cap to several people, including Treasurer Bill Thompson and his wife, Dottie, who helped run the emergency relief efforts at the township hall.

And then there are hundreds of tree cutters and debris-removal truck drivers. People like "Tree Top" Mike Conlan in Williamsburg and Larsen and Yensen Schwab and Rich Murrell with Unlimited Outdoors in Rapid City who worked 12– to 14-hour days to get trees off homes and garages and open blocked driveways.

Hats off to you all!

Photo by Michele Aucello

Photo by Michele Aucello

Photo by JoAnne Rodgers

Photo by Donna Kaplowitz

Photo by Beth Hobbes Chiles

Photo by Derold Stanton

**Old Mission Peninsula,
Grand Traverse County
Photo by Gwen MacDonald**
The storm cloud as it looked sweeping over Chateau Grand Traverse, one of the few Old Mission wineries that was open for business the next day.

**Elk Rapids, Antrim County
Photo by Travis Bratschi**
Hail ruined Travis Bratschi's 2015 apple crop.

**Old Mission Peninsula,
Grand Traverse County
Photo by Bonobo Winery**
Vine and grape damage at Bonobo.

O n Old Mission Peninsula, Bonobo Winery was packed with visitors sampling the new business's emblematic chardonnays. Owner Todd Oosterhouse was looking ahead to Monday, Aug. 3, when his vineyard team would peel back the leaves on 18 acres of vines to expose clusters of white grapes to begin the ripening process.

On Elk Lake Road, Travis Bratschi was tinkering in his apple farm shop, encouraged that he would soon reap his first significant harvest and be able to pay the bills to keep his young apple operation afloat. He and his wife, Erin, and children, Samuel and Sophie, soon piled in the car and headed to his brother's home for Sunday dinner.

Within an hour, first striking Old Mission and then the orchards between East Bay and Elk Lake, the vicious bow echo-driven thunderstorm began spitting iceballs and churning up mighty winds.

Suddenly, life changed for Oosterhouse and Bratschi and dozens of others who own vineyards, orchards and farms in Leelanau, Grand Traverse and Antrim counties.

"The apple crop was a total loss. All these thoughts going through my mind," said Bratschi, who bought the land in 2010 and started planting apple trees the next year. "I have loans to pay and bills to pay. Then I thought, yes, I was grateful that everybody was safe."

Bratschi grew up in a family in the fruit business and knows the ups and downs. Now he knows he's way down. The wind broke branches; hundreds of unripened apples lay on the ground, and what remained on the young trees showed hail scars. Some might be worth picking for

VINEYARDS & ORCHARDS SUFFER
BY ROBERT CAMPBELL

cider or deer feed, but the high-value fruits were gone. A longer-term concern is scarring on the tree stems, making them more vulnerable to disease and infestation.

"It's like your boss coming to you and telling you you're not going to get your paycheck for 16 months," Bratschi said. "If we have a late frost next spring, I'll have no choice but to put the farm up for sale."

The last two years have been tough on vineyard and orchard owners. In 2014, the cold and relentless snows damaged many vines. In 2015, several days of extreme cold in February and hard frosts in late May hurt crops. The Aug. 2 storm was the third blow.

 e'll be lucky if we get any crop," Oosterhouse said. "We had been looking good, pretty strong. The next day we were going to pull leaves around the fruiting zones. But by Monday all the leaves were gone, all your nice clusters of fruit were gone. The hail was basically like machine-gun fire."

Immediately, he and his winemaker began making calls to growers on both U.S. coasts to find grapes to make wines for their tasting rooms and for the next year.

Most of the cherries in the areas hardest hit by the storm — which ripen during early to mid-July — already had been picked. Still, in one orchard on Lossie Road in Whitewater Township, the wind sheared off dozen of older cherry trees.

Meanwhile, many of the region's fast-growing number of hop farms, where the beer-making essential is grown, also suffered major damage. Duke Elsner, extension educator for small fruits and consumer horticulture at Michigan State University's Extension Service in Traverse City, estimated overall agricultural losses in the region as "many millions of dollars."

"It's going to be a real test of anyone's — particularly some of the smaller, newer operations — ability to hang in there."

Photo by Dierdre Dembowski

Photo by Michele Aucello

Photo by Ethan Barth

Photo by Tyler

Photo by Annie Rollo

Photo by Jennifer Szunko

Photo by Beth Hobbes Chiles

Photo by Steve Webb

Photo by Linda Stephan

Photo by Keith Burnham

Photo by Carol Vernam

Photo by Bridget Devin

Photo by Cheri Fettes

Photo by Stacy Knutson

Photo by Fran Housman

Photo by Tim Harbin

THIS BOOK STARTED WITH TWO EMAILS. Mission Point Press partner Doug Weaver wrote friend Bob Campbell, who lives on Skegemog Lake, a couple of days after Aug. 2, 2015.

"How did you guys fare with the storm?"

"We were slammed," Bob answered. "Seven trees across the driveway. One on the garage."

He went into considerable detail, but ended his email with: "Maybe there's a book here. People who've been here a lifetime say it's the worst they've ever seen."

A great idea. And Mission Point Press was off and running. In a meeting soon after, MPP partners Anne Stanton, Heather Lee Shaw and Weaver discussed the logistics. Decisions came fast:

MPP would approach Campbell, a retired political editor for the *Detroit Free Press*, to do the book's narrative. Bob jumped at it.

Photos would be a challenge. MPP couldn't easily hire one or two photographers to go out after the fact when cleanup was already well under way. "Crowd-source the photos," suggested Heather. Ask the pubic to submit their best pictures, and give a free book to people whose photos are selected. Another great idea! Bob Butz, an area writer and freelancer called during that first meeting, was asked to edit the submitted photos and captions. He agreed.

A book like this needs to do good: MPP quickly decided to donate some of the proceeds to the Friends of Sleeping Bear Dunes.

And one of the most eloquent observers of the destruction, Bob Sutherland, president and founder of Cherry Republic, was chronicling on his blog the devastation visited upon the Glen Arbor area. Why not ask Bob to provide the foreword? He agreed.

You are holding the result of this publishing effort. MPP thanks the three Bobs for their enthusiasm and hard work.

And hats off to the more than 70 photographers who contributed their dramatic pictures.

Finally, this book is dedicated to the community of residents and visitors — from Glen Arbor on the west to Skegemog Lake and beyond on the east — who did battle with the winds of Aug. 2, 2015.

Your courage, perseverance, humor and selflessness are an inspiration.

Perch Lake, Kalkaska County
Photo by Craig Goodrich
The day after the storm.